COUNTRIES IN THIS SERIES

THE SIMPLE GUIDE TO

HOLLAND

CUSTOMS & ETIQUETTE

COVER ILLUSTRATION

Assorted pairs of wooden clogs by Lou Jones. Courtesy Image Bank. [For afficionados of statistics, a cubic metre of wood is sufficient material for 50 pairs of clogs.]

ABOUT THE AUTHOR

MARK T. HOOKER served as a linguist and foreign area specialist with the US Armed Forces, and later as a Department of Defence civilian. He is currently a visiting scholar at Indiana University. His wife, Stella, was born and educated in The Hague. Their daughter Catherine attends school in Holland every summer.

ILLUSTRATED BY
IRENE SANDERSON

THE SIMPLE GUIDE TO

HOLLAND

CUSTOMS & ETIQUETTE

Mark T. Hooker

GLOBAL BOOKS LTD

Simple Guides · Series 1
CUSTOMS & ETIQUETTE

The Simple Guide to
HOLLAND
CUSTOMS & ETIQUETTE

First published 1997 by
Global Books Ltd
PO Box 219, Folkestone, Kent CT20 3LZ, England

© Global Books Ltd 1997

ISBN 1-86034-085-7

British Library Cataloguing in Publication Data
A CIP catalogue entry for this book
is available from the British Library.

Distributed in the USA & Canada by:
The Talman Co., Inc., New York

Set in Futura 11 on 12 pt by Bookman, Slough
Printed in Great Britain by
The Cromwell Press, Broughton Gifford, Wiltshire

Contents

MAP OF HOLLAND [THE NETHERLANDS]

INTRODUCTION
Dutch Icons

'Windmills, clogs, tulips . . .'

Holland is a land of windmills, clogs (wooden shoes), tulips and cheese. At least, that is what all the tourists see. But, as we shall see, there is a great deal more to these 'royal' lowlands than the conventional stereotypes suggest. So, first of all, let us examine each of these 'tourist attractions' on their merits.

Windmills are common in Holland, because the country is so flat that there is nothing to get in the wind's way and there is plenty of it coming off the North Sea. Nobody will argue with that! It is, therefore, a cheap, plentiful source of power. Windmills have long been a part of the Dutch battle to keep Holland above water. Placed on dikes, they were used to drive pumps. Because the maximum lift for a wind-driven pump is 1.5 metres (5 feet or 150 centimetres), you can often see a line of two or three windmills on a dike. Gradually, however, windmills were replaced – first, by steam-driven, and then by electric pumps. Nowadays, they are largely to be admired. Unless you like climbing narrow staircases with lots of steps and no bannister, make no mistake, they are best viewed from outside!

It is a fact that some people still continue to wear clogs in Holland, but you have to go to a living museum (like Volendam) or to a farm to find them. However, even though clogs are no longer a part of everyday life, they are still very much part of the language. For example, there are countless expressions relating to clogs, such as: 'Now that breaks my *klomp* (clog)' – meaning something very unusual, because clogs hardly ever break; or 'You can feel that through your *klompen* (clogs)' – meaning something is so obvious that you can feel it through your clogs, which are very good safety shoes.

Tulips, another icon of Holland, were originally imported to Holland from Turkey in the sixteenth century. Even the word tulip comes from the Turkish word for turban. The records show that in February 1637, the futures market in tulip bulbs collapsed as the price for deliveries of bulbs not yet harvested inflated to bursting point. In 1987, some two hundred-and-fifty years later, this event gained prominence again after the October mini-crash in the US stock market, when analysts used it as a historical example to explain what happened to the stock market. Tulip bulbs are still big business today. The flowers are just a by-product of raising the bulbs and are sold very cheaply in Holland.

The Belgians call the Dutch 'Cheese heads' because they eat so much cheese. But as much as they eat, they export even more. Ever practical-minded, the Dutch long ago learned that if you turned milk, which spoils quickly, into cheese, which does not, you could ship it long distances and sell it. In his description of Holland, published in 1567, Lodovico Guiccardini noted that Dutch cheese and butter were worth as much as all the spices imported from Portugal – several million guilders-worth a year. Gouda (a word that hardly anyone can pronounce correctly) is the name of one of the most famous cheeses in the world (some would say 'the' most famous!) So, surprise the shop assistant helping you buy some and pronounce the word correctly – '**how-dah**'.

Another great icon of Holland is Hans Brinker – the hero who put his finger in the dike to save a town from flooding. And as sure as you are that every Dutch(wo)man you meet in Holland knows the story of Hans Brinker, the Dutch are all sure that the rest of the world knows the stories of *Arendsoog* (Eagle Eye) and *Witte Veder* (White Feather). Hans Brinker was written in 1865 by the American writer, Mary Mapes Dodge (1831-1905), who had never been to Holland and made up the story of the little boy with his finger in the dike. Arendsoog and Witte Veder are the heroes of a series of 'western' novels for children written by Jan Nowee and his son Paul, who never set foot in America!

For English-speaking visitors to Holland it is easy to get the feeling that everything is just like it is at home, because everyone in Holland speaks English so well. In many ways (or not, as the case may be) things are much the same. Yet, it is the subtle little differences that perhaps neither you nor your Dutch acquaintances are fully aware of that can cause you the most trouble. That is what this book is about. And, by definition, it is also about getting so much more out of your visit(s), for business or pleasure, or indeed both.

M.T.H.
Spring 1997

Land, Sea & People

Seventeenth-century houses in Amsterdam

The official name of Holland is the Kingdom of the Netherlands. It is a constitutional monarchy about the size of the states of Massachusetts and Connecticut put together (13,097 square miles/ 41,526 square kilometres). Belgium is just a little smaller than the Netherlands, but Germany is nearly nine times its size.

Holland literally means 'land in a hollow'. On the other hand, the word 'Netherlands' refers to the low-lying nature of the country – 'nether' literally meaning 'low'. Nearly 25 per cent of the country is below sea level, and that is where about 60 per cent of the population lives. The average elevation is only 37 feet (11 metres). Holland is so low because it covers the deltas of three rivers – the Rhine, the Maas and the Scheldt – where they flow into the North Sea. The lowest point, near Rotterdam, is some 6.7 metres (22 feet) below sea level. Because there is water everywhere you go, swimming is a required subject in primary school as a practical safety measure.

Top Tip

The fight to keep the low lands above water has been long and hard. Dutch character reflects that struggle. The Dutch people are hard-working, determined and do not give up easily.

THE AFSLUITDIJK

The Afsluitdijk (the Closing Dike), a 32-kilometre-long barrier dam that joins the provinces of North Holland and Friesland, was completed in 1932. It closed off the North Sea from the Zuyder Zee (zee = sea), and transformed it into an inland sea, which gradually became a freshwater lake, known as the IJsselmeer (meer = lake). It is viewed by the Dutch as a monument to their success in the constant struggle to keep nature in check and keep their land above water.

In addition to the protection it offers from flooding, the Afsluitdijk made it possible to drain parts of the IJsselmeer, and turn them into what the Dutch call polders (land reclaimed from under the water).

The IJsselmeer polders have added 1650 square kilometres (637 square miles) to the land mass of Holland.

The last major natural challenge to the dam was in February 1953, but the Afsluitdijk held. Nevertheless, flooding covered some 1500 square kilometres (579 square miles) with the loss of 1853 lives among people living in the south of Holland. The Dutch reaction was a major water control project called the Delta Works, which is still not fully completed. Even though the Delta Works are far advanced, the Dutch have not yet won their battle against the sea. The Afsluitdijk and the Delta Works focused on the danger of flooding from the sea, but in February 1995 rising rivers in the south of the country were the danger. The government swiftly took action to improve flood control on this front as well.

Holland was originally the name of a county of the Holy Roman Empire, that was part of Lotharingria (Lorraine). It became independent in 1018. It was inhabited by the Fresians who now live on the coast in Northern Holland in the province of Friesland. It was located about where the provinces of North and South Holland are today: centred around Amsterdam and the Hague. Theirs is the dialect of Dutch that is closest to English. As an English-speaker, I have less trouble understanding Frisian dialect than the Dutch do, because of all the similarities to English.

Prince William of Orange (1533-84)

It was from a base in what is now North and South Holland that William of Orange – the first in line of the present royal house of the Netherlands – waged his successful campaign for independence against Philip II of Spain, to whom Holland belonged as a part of the Hapsburg possessions. When peace was finally declared in 1648 (the Peace of Westphalia) Spain recognized what is now Holland (including Zeeland and Utrecht) as a free republic, but maintained its hold on the southern half of the country, which is now a part of Belgium.

NEW YORK AND THE DUTCH

The Dutch were the first to settle what today is known as New York. In 1609 Henry Hudson, after whom the Hudson River is named, sailed into New York Bay, looking for a northern passage to India. Because Hudson was working for the Dutch East India Company, Holland claimed the land there. It was Peter Minuit, the governor of the colony of the 'New Netherlands', who officially bought the entire island of Manhattan from the Indians for 60 guilders worth of trade goods.

In 1664 – ten years after the end of the War of 1652-54 between England and Holland – King Charles II of England 'gave' the New Netherlands to his brother, the Duke of York. He sent an expeditionary force to the colony to make sure that his gift did not change its mind. Dutch colonial policy had been primarily directed at the establishment of trading posts and not the creation of permanent settlements. In the last year of Dutch control (1664) there were approximately 10,000 inhabitants in the colony, not nearly enough to successfully defend it against British troops. When peace was again restored between the two countries in 1667, the New Netherlands was officially surrendered to England in exchange for Suriname in north-eastern South America.

If Holland could have held onto the New Netherlands, things would have been very different these days and not just in present-day New York state. Given the Dutch policy on colonial settlement and interaction with the local population, there would have been a lot more Iroquois in the New Netherlands. Things would have been quite different in Holland as well. In 1974/5, following Suriname's independence, substantial numbers of Surinamese emigrated to Holland, resulting today in a total Surinamese population (first and second generations) of some 300,000, or about 2% of the Dutch population. There is many a Dutchman – though few would admit it in public – who believes that absorbing such numbers amounted to a bridge too far. On the other hand, accommodating the Iroquois would not necessarily have been any easier. In any event, the year 1975 signalled a major change in Holland's ethnic make-up.

'DUTCH COURAGE'

It was out of the fierce struggle for economic supremacy between England and Holland in the seventeenth century that the large number of pejorative phrases that begin with the word 'Dutch' took root in the English language. The poem written by the English poet Edmund Waller (1606-87), celebrating the victory of the British fleet over the Dutch on 3 June 1665 was one of the first written uses of 'Dutch courage':

> *The Dutch their wine and brandy lose,*
> *Disarmed of that from which their courage grows.*

This war propaganda outlived the war itself and took on a life of its own.

Dutch courage is the kind that comes out of a bottle

Dutch treat is an invitation to a dinner that you have to pay for

Dutch reckoning is guesswork

a **Dutch nightingale** is a frog

a **Dutch auction** is where the asking price begins high and goes down

going Dutch is when two people or more people split the cost of something (usually a meal) between them

This is just a sample of the inventiveness of English propagandists. There were many more besides, most of which have finally fallen into disuse.

Between 1689 and 1713, the Dutch and the English formed a coalition against Louis XIV of France. The burden of defence expenditures associated with the coalition were too much for the Dutch republic and the peace of Utrecht (1713) saw Dutch international influence on the decline. Their financial problems had been worsened by the shift in the world economy from a purely mercantile base to an industrial base. The Dutch only had services to offer and were dependent on international seaborne trade to keep their economy afloat. The English industrial base allowed the British to finally gain the upper hand in their long economic struggle.

In the Napoleonic period, the Dutch were taken over by the French between 1795 and 1813, but in 1814 the Kingdom of the Netherlands came into being, encompassing the present-day Netherlands, Belgium and Luxembourg. In 1830, however, the Southern Netherlands, as it was then called, seceded and formed the country of Belgium.

Heading the monarchy today is Queen Beatrix who succeeded to the throne in 1980 following the abdication of her mother Queen Juliana who, in turn, became queen following her mother Wilhelmina's abdication in 1948 after a reign of 50 years.

Dutch Tolerance

Rembrandt's self-portrait as the Apostle Paul

The Dutch, in general, do not like surprises. That is what the system of rules and regulations that bind Dutch society so tightly are there for – to keep down the number of surprises. In any country as crowded as Holland, surprises are an inevitable part of everyday life when so many people compete to use the same space. (There is a population of over 15 million with about 470 people per square kilometre/1221 per square mile, making it one of the world's most densely-populated countries.)

The idea of regulations may seem out of character with a society where the kinds of things that are considered controversial in other societies, such as soft-drug 'Coffee Shops', gay marriages and euthanasia, are possible, but in Holland, all these things are controlled by the regulations. The regulations try to balance reducing the amount of confrontation with preserving an individual's freedom of thought and life-style.

Top Tip

The Dutch are all realists, which is why every Dutchman has so many insurance policies – to mitigate the effect of a surprise whenever it comes along.

The limits of tolerance are defined in the regulations to keep whatever 'strange' thing you want to do from bothering someone else. If you do bother someone else, your actions become intolerable. The word that the Dutch use for this situation is quite insightful. They call it: *overlast*. If your behaviour is only inconvenient, it is *lastig*, and they will put up with it. But, when it becomes overly inconvenient, it is *overlast*, and steps are taken to eliminate it. That is increasingly becoming the attitude of people who live near 'Coffee Shops', and people who have to deal with non-European foreigners a lot.

The Dutch 'blind eye' policy on the soft drugs trade at 'Coffee Shops' is testing the limits of tolerance, not because of people's revulsion at the thought of using soft drugs, but because of the *overlast* for those who live nearby, created by the Coffee Shops' clientele.

Foreigners are treated with Dutch politeness, which, when compared to other versions of decorum, may seem rather standoffish. It was one of the factors that made the Pilgrim Fathers leave Holland for America. The Dutch were prepared to offer them religious freedom and tolerance within the framework of rules that makes up Dutch society, but the Pilgrims felt constrained by that and left Holland in 1620 after 11 years of living in Leiden to establish the Plymouth colony in Massachusetts.

Top Tip

The Dutch still welcome foreigners with different ideas and religions, just as they did the Pilgrims in the seventeenth century. Today, they even offer resident aliens the right to vote in local elections, and parliament has gone as far as debating whether to give them voting rights in the national parliamentary elections as well.

Growing Dutch intolerance of foreigners these days is due in great part to the growing numbers of foreigners moving into Holland who, like the Pilgrims, find the strict Dutch rules too binding. To the mind of many Dutch people, today's foreigners, unlike the Pilgrims, are insisting that the Dutch change their way of life to accommodate them, rather than the other way round. The old axiom of *when in Rome, do as the Romans*, holds as true today as ever it did, and not just in Holland.

The Dutch are not necessarily disturbed by new ideas, but are somewhat reluctant to try them out themselves. The Dutch are exposed to new ideas all the time. Because of their multiple language skills (English and German are the most common, with French a distant third), they are exposed to a wide variety of ideas from the foreign media. In Holland, you can listen to AM radio direct from Germany, England, Belgium, Scandinavia and France. Foreign TV reception is not limited to those near the border, inside the coverage area of foreign TV stations. A basic cable TV subscription includes German, French, Italian, British and Belgian, as well as the Dutch public (state-owned) and commercial stations.

American TV shows probably have the most impact, because they have the highest exposure on Dutch TV. You can actually log the extent of this cultural import by listening to the spoken language. Any number of American words and phrases, such as 'in the picture', 'hurry up', and 'shit!' seem to pepper Dutch conversations, yet the people using them appear to be barely conscious, if at all, that they are not Dutch words.

While the ideas contained in the foreign media get at least a tolerant reception, TV commercials are met with a high degree of hostility. A great many Dutch people, simply cannot understand how anyone could possibly put up with so many interruptions during the course of the broadcast; they complain frequently and loudly about it.

On one occasion, there was a great deal of dissatisfaction when the national soccer league sold the broadcast rights to its games to a commercial network, because people were afraid that the commercial 'interruptions' would spoil their enjoyment of the game. There were so many problems with this deal that the network was driven into bankruptcy. There are commercials on Dutch non-commercial TV, but they are grouped together in between the News and Prime Time. When they come in (it is a ten-minute slot), most people just turn off the sound and go off to do something else.

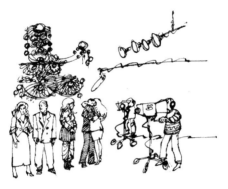

Dutch TV game shows are very popular

Dutch non-commercial TV is funded from TV viewing licence fees. The airtime on the three non-commercial channels and funding are apportioned to the eight TV networks, based – following the parliamentary model – on the number of members that they have. Viewers who have paid their TV viewing licence can become members of one or more networks by subscribing to that network's TV Guide. Each network's TV Guide lists all the shows carried by the other networks, but has more detailed coverage of its own shows.

Top Tip

Each of the Dutch TV networks has its own specific ideas and philosophy to advance with its programming. The EO, for example, provides programmes to suit the tastes of Protestant religious conservatives. The KRO has traditionally been the Catholic voice on radio and TV. The members of the VARA have Socialist interests. This approach to TV programming keeps a wide variety of ideas and philosophies in the public eye – so to speak.

3

Home & Family

A traditional example of 'Gezelligheid'

Gezelligheid is the feeling of being together with family and friends in comfortable surroundings. Gezelligheid seems to be lubricated with coffee. Indeed, one gets the impression that there always seems to be coffee waiting to be poured.

The Dutch equivalent of 'Time flies when you're having fun' is Gezelligheid kent geen tijd (Cosiness is not aware of the time). Children, who have not yet mastered complex abstract nouns can be heard trying to reproduce this proverb as *Een gezellige geit kent geen tijd* (A friendly goat is not aware of the time).

The Dutch have another sense of distance. It is defined by the size of the country they live in. In Holland, hearing the way people perceive distance, you would think that they lived on the other side of the world! For example, a two-hour drive away, for whatever reason – including getting to a family event, is considered a major decision in Holland. Whereas, in America, you might well drive two hours to eat at a restaurant you like, and your parents live two time zones away. The feeling of a Dutch family in the Hague whose son moved to Groningen (three hours away by train) in the North of Holland is the same as an American family in Alabama, whose son has moved to California (five hours by plane and three times zones away).

When they go away to college, if they do not live at home, children are most likely to be found at home at the weekend. As noted above, the sense of family is therefore much stronger in Holland than in America or Britain. The Dutch simply spend more time at home and have more contact with their families.

You can see that interpersonal relationships are family-centred by the way that personal – not business or junk – mail is addressed. Correspondence goes to the van Dijk family, not to Hans and Mieke van Dijk. On the inside, there will be a salutation to everyone in the family. The letter will close with best wishes from everyone in the family that sent the letter. Individual signatures are preferred, but, at a pinch, one person can sign for the whole family, one name at a time.

'Open house'

The curtains in Dutch houses are open during the day so that you can look inside. In a row of town houses, you can normally see all the way through into the back garden. The Dutch always say that this is a carry-over from the Second World War years when all the curtains had to be closed tight because of air-raids; but if you listen to the comments that people make when they pass by an open window and look inside, it is clear that they are measuring the inhabitant's compliance with the rules of polite society.

The view from the street is usually of the living-room and dining-room – the bedrooms and bathrooms being on the upper floors. Everything inside will be neat and tidy. The people, if they are at home, invariably will be as well dressed as if they were just about to go into town.

Top Tip

Woe betide those who do not open their curtains for inspection each day! They are immediately suspected of all sorts of breaches of decorum. It is very much like living in a goldfish bowl!

4

Festivals & Holiday Traditions

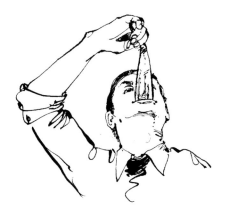

Enjoying raw herring

NEW YEAR'S EVE

The change from the old year to the new is celebrated with a massive explosion of fireworks throughout the country set off by individuals welcoming in the new year. In 1995, 30 million guilders was spent on New Year's fireworks. Despite a considerable number of firework-related injuries, the tradition continues. It is safest to watch from inside.

Typical treats for this time of year are: *Appel-flappen* – fried, battered apple rings and *Oliebollen* – hole-less doughnuts filled with raisins, deep-fried in oil and dipped in powdered sugar. Be sure to try one of each.

APRIL FOOL'S DAY

Practical jokes on 1 April are elevated to an art form. Almost all the print and electronic media take part in the fun by covering a 'story' that later turns out to be an April Fool's joke. And everyone makes it their business to be the first to spot the 'April Fool'.

VPRO Radio (the Liberal Protestant Radio Network) once 'covered' a strange affliction that had struck Rembrandt's 'The Night Watch'. The paint had begun to peel off slowly but surely and the whole image was expected to vanish by approximately midnight. The National Gallery would reopen at eight that night so that art-lovers country-wide could cast one last glance at the famous painting. Just before eight, there was a considerable crowd in front of the museum. It was not until the reporters from VPRO Radio began to interview them, that the crowd caught on that this was a gigantic April Fool's joke.

THE QUEEN'S BIRTHDAY

The Queen's Birthday is a major celebration. It is observed on 30 April. This is not Queen Beatrix's birthday, but the Queen Mother's – Juliana's. When Beatrix ascended the throne, the Dutch decided to leave the official celebration on the Queen Mother's birthday. In doing so, they continued to honour the Queen Mother, and avoided moving the holiday to January, which is much too cold for most of the outdoor activities that accompany the occasion.

The royal birthday is a bank holiday celebrated by fairs and open-air markets. The whole country is decked with red, white and blue national flags and orange ensigns, which honour the Royal Family – the House of Orange. Each year, as part of the day's festivities, the Queen and her family pay an official visit to two towns, where she is received with full pomp and circumstance.

BIRTHDAYS

Not just the Queen's birthday, but everybody's birthday is a big event in Holland. Every Dutch home has a birthday calendar hanging in the bathroom so that you can see it every time you sit down to respond to the call of nature. It is there to remind you of the upcoming birthdays of all the family's friends and relations, all of which will be observed in one way or another. At the very least there will be a card addressed to the *jarige* – the birthday celebrant. This salutation alerts family members to the fact that it is a birthday card that is to be put aside and delivered on the day itself. For close family and friends, a visit is called for.

Top Tip

The Dutch do not send out birthday party invitations. It is assumed there will be a party unless people are notified otherwise. Actually, it will be more like an open house than a party. Guests come in small groups throughout the day, often calling in advance to reserve a time. Coffee and pastries are brought out as each new guest arrives.

Presents do not have to be expensive. It is the thought that counts. Practical to a fault, many Dutch families follow the custom of keeping a wishlist near the telephone in the weeks before someone's birthday. When people call to find out what time is convenient to come, they also ask what is on the list. That way they do not duplicate someone else's present and the celebrant gets what he or she wants.

AUCTION OF THE FIRST HERRING CATCH

The first catch of the season is celebrated with great ceremony at the end of May. The Queen is offered the *Koninginneharing* – the best one of the catch, and the first barrel of herring is auctioned off, with the proceeds going to charity.

Herring are dipped in diced onions and eaten raw. It is somewhat of an acquired taste, but one that any visitor to Holland at this time of year will be encouraged to try. You hold the herring (don't call it a fish!) by its tail, dip it in the onions, tilt your head back, dangle the herring over your mouth and take a bite.

5 DECEMBER

Saint Nicholas, the Dutch ancestor of Santa Claus, comes on 5 December to bring presents. The Saint Nicholas season begins on the Saturday nearest 11 November, when he arrives by steam-boat from Spain, where he lives with his retinue of Black Peters.

Families with small children, who still believe these things, arrange a visit from the 'Good Holy Man', as Saint Nicholas is called. When he arrives at the home, Black Peter bangs on the door loudly and throws a handful of *pepernoten* (ginger-bread buttons) into the room before Saint Nicholas enters. As Saint Nicholas gives out each present, he reads out the entry in his Big Book about the person receiving it.

Adults celebrating without children prepare what are known as *surprises*. *Surprises* are very elaborate, large packages for small presents. They are accompanied by a rhyme that pokes fun at the recipient. The rhyme is signed by *Ide Sint* (The Saint) and the identity of the real giver is supposed to remain a mystery. As evening approaches on 5 December, it is not unusual to see people getting onto trams or buses with colourful, large paper-maché objects like bass fiddles or computers or cars. They are on their way to a surprise party!

The celebration of 5 December has come under some commercial pressure to shift present-giving to Christmas, where studies have shown that the presents given on Christmas Day are bigger and more expensive. In some municipalities, people are fighting back, however, to preserve what is a very uniquely Dutch celebration. Some cities have outlawed the use of Christmas motifs in advertising and appearances by Santa Claus until 6 December, the day that Saint Nicholas leaves Holland to return to Spain.

5

Eating Out

Vrijthof terrace at Maastricht

Under the Dutch 'blind eye' soft drugs policy, (p. 22), 'Coffee Shops' can sell customers up to five grams of cannabis for personal use. Unless that is what you are looking for, therefore, do not drop into a 'Coffee Shop'. If you want a cup of coffee and a piece of very delicious Dutch apple pie, go to a cafe, a snack-bar, or cafeteria instead.

As noted earlier (p. 28), the Dutch are very much home bodies. They do not go out often, but when they do they dress up to the nines and make the most of it. When you do go out to dinner at a restaurant, therefore, it can be an expensive, long, drawn-out experience. The service is not rushed so as to provide the guest with time to enjoy the occasion which (s)he is paying for. If you are in a hurry or just looking for food and not a dining experience, try a cafeteria in a large department store, or an *afhaalcentrum* (take-away centre) with tables.

Of course, there are snack-bars where you can grab a quick bite to eat, but you do not see a lot of families there. Families usually send someone out to a snack-bar for take-away fast-food and eat it at home with the family, where it is *gezellig* (cosy).

SNACK-BAR FOOD

Some of the food that you find in a Dutch snack-bar requires explanation:

PATAT (French fries/chips) are easy enough to understand, but what do you put on them? Not ketchup or vinegar, but *frietsaus* (mayonnaise) or *pindasaus* (spicy, Indonesian peanut sauce). Both are quite delicious and are well worth trying. Although hardly any snack-bars produce their own sauces, the *pindasaus* varies more in taste than the *frietsaus*, so that while you may not like it at one place, you may find it quite agreeable at another. French fries can be eaten with fingers, but the more fastidious customers use the little plastic forks that you can pick up at the counter.

KROKETTEN (croquettes) are essentially a Dutch speciality. They are shaped like a short hot dog, but are made from a soft, meat-based filling, covered in breadcrumbs and fried. They are best eaten with *mosterd* (mustard), either straight from hand to mouth, or with a knife and fork. Cutlery is recommended not so much because it is more elegant, but because *kroketten* are very hot when served and just biting straight into one can be a very unpleasant experience for your mouth. Cutting the *kroketten* open down the centre and then spreading on the mustard gives them time to cool off before you take the first bite!

BITTERBALLEN (bitter balls) are just *kroketten* served as bite-sized balls instead of as short hot dogs. They are quite popular as snacks at parties. They are even hotter than regular *kroketten* when served, so be sure to let them cool off a bit before you put them into your mouth.

NASIBALLEN (fried rice balls) are an attempt at making a portable snack out of an Indonesian dish that is popular in Holland. They are about the size of a tennis ball, though are not as chewy, and not nearly as tasty as the dish they try to emulate. Get the real thing instead!

A better alternative to snack-bar food is take-away from a Chinese or Indonesian restaurant. This option is so popular that, similar to Britain, many restaurants have special-waiting-rooms near the kitchen for their take-away customers so that people can pick up food without bothering the eat-in guests. When you go to the kitchen for your take-away instead of ordering in the restaurant, the prices are usually lower.

If you have the time, try a *rijsttafel* (rice table). It is a sampler of Indonesian food. The portions are small, but the more elaborate rice tables can run to 40 or more dishes. Do not hesitate to ask what each dish is – especially if you like it. The waiters will be happy to explain each one.

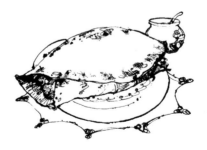

Pancake – Dutch-style

A *Pannekoekhuis* (pancake house) is a uniquely Dutch experience. The pancakes hang over

the sides of the 13-inch plates they are served on –
one to a plate. Pancakes with syrup and sugar are
readily available, but they are hardly the only thing
on the menu. Most of the menu items are a real
meal. Try a ham-and-cheese pancake or one with
something even more exotic. These huge creations
are a lot of food, so go along with an empty
stomach, if you plan to order one.

If you do order a sweet pancake, it is becoming
more common to find syrup on the table, but the
Dutch prefer *stroop* (molasses). It is usually made
from sugar beets, but you can also get apple
stroop, which is well worth tasting. The other most
common sweet topping is *poedersuiker* (powdered
sugar).

On the other hand, if you are just looking for a
snack, order *poffertjes* (silver-dollar pancakes). These are as much fun to watch being
made as they are to eat. They are cooked on a
special griddle that is not flat, but is covered with
little round indentations that make it look like a non-
slip floor for giants. The batter is poured into each
hole in turn and the cook flips the *poffertjes* with a
fork. It is quite a show. Many pancake houses have
the *poffertjes* griddle set up behind a glass wall so
you can watch how it is done.

TIPPING

Tipping: Do not tip at a snack-bar or *afhaalcentrum*. In an establishment with table service,
15% is customary if the service was good. You
announce the tip to the server when he comes to
collect the bill, by telling him how much to keep or

how much change you want back. Never leave your tip on the table.

6

Shopping

Market day in Haarlem

There is no shortage of shopping malls in Holland. In fact, the world's first mall was built in Holland in 1953. Shopping in a chain store in a Dutch mall is much like shopping in a chain store in a mall anywhere. The only real major differences are the use of e-money and the Dutch gift-wrapping tradition.

The Dutch lead the rest of Europe in the use of e-money. The Dutch *PIN* (pay with e-money) almost everywhere. You can, too, but you will need the PIN (Personal Identification Number) that goes with your credit or debit card to verify that you are its owner. You have to punch it in at the point of sale. Know the numbers, not the word that the bank gives you to help you remember it. Dutch number pads for *PIN*-ing do not have letters on them.

Especially around 5 December (Saint Nicholas' Day), shop assistants will ask you: *Is het een cadeautje?* (is et 'n kado-che? – 'che' rhyming with 'chest' – 'is it a present?') when you pay for your purchase. If you indicate that it is, they will take off the price sticker and wrap it in pretty paper. At other times of the year, the staff may not ask you, but you can certainly have your purchase wrapped then as well by telling the clerk: *het is een cadeautje* (et is 'n kado-che).

There is a weekly open-air market in almost every town. Cheese, bread, fruits and vegetables are what you would expect, but you will also find bicycle parts, clothing, reading glasses, greeting cards, pastry and sweets, garden goods, pots and pans, shoes, souvenirs, poultry, Indonesian spices, fish and computer software. All in direct competition with the permanent stores in the immediate vicinity. The products and prices are almost the same as in the stores, but the atmosphere is different. The street is alive with people, sounds and smells. There are samples to taste before you buy.

The weekly market does not have the fly-by-night atmosphere of a flea market, where you buy things that fell off the back of a lorry. Both the customers and the people working in the stalls know each other by name. These are the same people, week after week, month after month, year after year, in the same spot, rain, snow, sleet and dark of night on the short days of winter in Northern Europe.

The advertising slogan 'at the market, your guilder is worth a *daalder* (one guilder fifty)' was truer some years ago than it is today. The expansion of supermarkets with their economies of scale and discounts for bulk purchases have closed the gap in price that the vendors at the market once enjoyed. You can still get good deals at the market just before closing time, when it is easier to sell the last pound of bananas at cost than to pack them up and take them home.

The other advantage of the market over the permanent stores – that of a low fixed over-head – is also being eroded by rising charges for market-stall space that are levied by the local municipal governments. Many of these family businesses are fast disappearing because these days parents discourage their children from following in their footsteps.

Haggling is not customary at the market. Unfortunately, you have to look out for pickpockets at markets in the larger cities.

In between the mall and the market are the small neighbourhood stores. The prices are usually higher than at the market or in the mall, but the service is better than in the mall and the smile about

'Shopping by bike is still quite common'

46

as big as you will find at the market. Supermarkets charge for bags to put your purchases in. Being as economy-minded as they are, the Dutch want to avoid this unnecessary expense, so most people carry their own shopping bags.

Even though supermarkets are becoming ever more prominent, many people still shop at more than one store. Since shopping on foot or by bike is still quite common, it is not unusual for a customer to have something in his or her shopping bag that is sold in the store they are in, but which was purchased at another store. If you shop like the Dutch do, always keep your cash register receipts! A number of stores ask to look inside your bag at the check-out and they will want to see the cash register receipts too.

Top Tip

Supermarkets and drug stores often require you to use a shopping trolley or basket while in the store. If you have your own shopping bag, use a trolley instead of a basket. The trolley has a hook on the front from which to hang your shopping bag. Its use is obligatory in some stores.

7

Visiting Formalities

'Kaffie?'

The Dutch do not like informal company to stop by at the drop of a hat, just because you were 'in the neighbourhood'. If you are on extremely good terms with someone, you can call in the morning to ask if you can pop in that evening, but normally you should call further in advance. The greater the social distance between you, the longer you need to call in advance. Children even call their parents – and vice versa – to see if it is all right if they come and visit.

Since the Dutch do not like 'surprise' company, when you arrive, the coffee will be ready to pour. Yours should be, too. An offer of coffee is the absolute minimum required by politeness when you invite someone into your home. Even the workmen, who come to fix a leaky tap, will be offered a cup of coffee and from the good china, not the everyday crockery the family uses. There will also be biscuits, or if it is a special occasion like a birthday or anniversary, pastries.

A couple known to us, who speak no Dutch, went to visit friends in Holland and when they came back, they were proud to announce that they had learned the Dutch word for 'Hello'. '*Koffie?*' he said with no accent at all, and he was right. The first thing any Dutch host(ess) says when someone comes into the house is not 'Hello', but: '*Koffie?*' (Would you like a cup of coffee?)

When you visit someone's home, always take a hospitality present. Flowers, bicsuits, or sweets are almost always appropriate. Your present may be opened on the spot and offered to you with the coffee, so make sure that you like what you are taking! Dutch chocolate, by the way, comes in two sorts: *puur* (bitter) and *melk* (milk). It probably does not matter to your host which kind you bring. Buy the kind you like. The packages are colour-coded: bitter is red and blue is milk.

When you visit Dutch friends at home, the arrival ritual is very important. Ladies enter first to a round of three – the number is significant – kisses on the cheek (right-left-right) with each person there. The men follow, shaking hands with the men and kissing all the ladies lightly on the cheek three times (right-left-right).

Family occasions are observed almost religiously. Everyone does their best to attend birthdays, anniversaries, weddings and graduations, etc. Not only is the celebrant congratulated on the occasion, but so are his or her parents, brothers and sisters, aunts and uncles, children and spouse.

'Remembering birthdays!'

If you are invited to someone's birthday party, do not just buy a present at random. Call ahead and reserve a present from their *lijstje* (list). Even though the celebrant made up the list, you do not want to ask them. That would spoil the 'surprise'. Talk instead to close friends or family and join in the 'conspiracy' to get what the celebrant wants.

Sometimes, for a very special occasion (silver anniversary, fiftieth birthday), there may be just one expensive present instead of a lot of small, inexpensive ones, which is usually the case. In that event, well-wishers usually split the price of the present, rather than buy something themselves. How much you pay depends on how many people call up beforehand to ask to be included. Whoever actually buys the present will tell you what your share of the price is at the party. You can pay them afterwards. A direct deposit to their bank is usually the preferred way.

The length of the pause between speakers in a Dutch conversation is a lot shorter than in English. Even when they speak English, the Dutch still use the same short pause to give others a chance to join the conversation. Until you get used to it, you may not get much said, because you do not recognize the shorter pause as a signal for someone else to say something. You may also, mistakenly, get the impression that all the people in the conversation are constantly interrupting each other. They aren't. It is just that the cue to change speakers is a lot shorter.

Top Tip

If your host invites you to watch something on TV, do not be surprised if the conversation continues throughout the show. The Dutch will be following the action by reading the subtitles, not by listening to the sound track. For them it is quite easy to read and talk at the same time. Their conversation will not be disturbed by the dialogue that you need to hear to keep up with the programme. Listen to the conversation and not the TV show, and try not to let the latter bother you.

The same Dutch tendency to engage in conversation regardless of the context may happen even when you go to the cinema. Don't be surprised if you find yourself surrounded by people having a conversation instead of watching the film. It can be extremely irritating, but there is not much that you can do about it; but forewarned is forearmed.

8

Business Matters

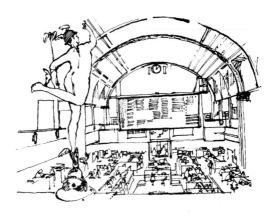

Amsterdam Stock Exchange

Because they speak English so well, it is easy to fall into the trap of thinking that the Dutch also do business the same way we do in America, or elsewhere in the English-speaking world. They are more reserved than Americans, and also the British to some extent. This is because the Dutch use social distance to make up for the lack of physical distance that they have in their small and crowded country. There are unwritten rules for what is polite and what is not. If you are polite, you get the deal. If you are not, you don't.

Top Tip

The Dutch favour a team effort and shun overly conspicuous individual achievement. The emphasis is on unlimited politeness, consensus-building, the regulation of social interaction, public reserve, and a high degree of tolerance for differences within a well-developed set of social traditions.

RULES OF THE GAME

- Formality is important. It is not only what you say, but how you say it. Not only what you wear, but how you wear it that makes an impression.

- The use of academic degrees and titles is expected in correspondence. Every Dutch personal planner has a list of titles and whom they are appropriate for. Letters sent to someone whose business card bears the title 'drs'. *(Doctorandus* – broadly equivalent to the American Master of Arts degree), for example – should be addressed to: *Weledelgeleerde Heer* . . . *Vrouwe* – (The Nobly Well Educated Lord . . . Lady) plus their initials and last name. The Dutch, however, do not take this as far as the Austrians and the Germans. The use of titles is not appropriate when speaking to the person face to face.

- Americans especially should avoid their natural tendency to address everyone by their first name. When you do that you are invading a Dutchman's social space. It is roughly equivalent to talking to another American with your nose three inches from theirs.

- Business appointments should be made in advance. The Dutch do not like surprises except when 'Sint Nikolaas' comes!

- Punctuality is very important. Arrive on time for meetings and ensure that deadlines and delivery dates are met. Always allow yourself lots of extra time to get to appointments. Traffic in Holland is notoriously bad, but getting stuck in it is no excuse for being late to a meeting. Deadlines and delivery dates should be pushed back in the initial negotiations to allow for unforeseen delays. An early delivery is much better than a late one or than trying to change a date once it is agreed upon.

- Introductions and an exchange of business cards should take place before the meeting begins. If you have a university degree or other title, put it on your card. Ensure that your card lists your initials and not your first name, middle initial. Professionally printed cards are preferred. Do not use the kind you can print yourself on a laser printer.

- Respond promptly to all correspondence, even if it is only to say that there will be a delay in providing the information requested.

- The Dutch prefer to establish long-term working relationships, which can best be supported by regular communications and periodic personal visits to your Dutch business contacts and trading partners. This shows your commitment to doing business with them over the long term.

Business in Holland is not conducted in a freewheeling environment – as it is in the United States. There are rules for everything. Anything you want to do needs a permit and every permit needs a diploma. This can be a daunting experience for foreigners trying to do business in Holland, but the Dutch are used to the rules and do not give up as easily as others. They know how to bend the rules when they have to, because everyone is sure that the exception to the rule – and there are always a few – applies to them.

The rules help the Dutch cope with life in a small, crowded country. If you follow all the rules, however, you may never get anything done. 'Zeg 'ns Aaaa', a popular Dutch TV sitcom that was a good mirror of Dutch everyday life, did a show in which one of the main characters, Koos, is contrasted to a building contractor, who followed all the rules. The contractor was bankrupt, had a broken arm and his wife had left him. Koos, on the other hand, was getting along well enough, bending the rules and making a living exploiting the black economy.

The normal reaction when a Dutchman encounters a new rule is to exclaim: 'Het zou toch moeten kunnen' ('this should really be possible'). People who bend the rules are looked up to and down on at the same time. When people found out that the owner of a major restaurant chain had large numbers of employees working for him but evading taxes, the comments were a sarcastic combination of jealousy and annoyance. 'I guess you have to be somebody to get away with that.'

Every rule has an exception and every Dutchman knows it. You only have to look at traffic signs as you go about the city to see how rampant it is. **'No Entry!** (Except for cyclists)' says one. **'No Parking!** (Except for permit holders)' says another. And you do not have to look for long to find that a dog had recently visited a 'curb-your-dog' sign built into the pavement.

The ultimate explicit statement that there is no exception to a rule is a physical barrier to make it impossible to do what the rule prohibits. If you really are not supposed to drive up a small country lane for any reason, there is a post in the middle of it that blocks your way and a sign below the **No Entry!** sign, warning you that there is a 'Post In The

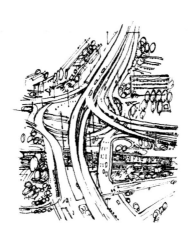

Road rules – Kleinpolderplein, Rotterdam

Road'. If you really cannot park here for any reason, there are posts along the curbside of the pavement half a car length apart and only one lane of traffic. If you are really not supposed to jump this red light or speed on this street, there is a camera on a post to take your picture while you do it, and automatically send you a fine. If you are really not supposed to walk on this wall, the top is built on a sixty-degree angle. If you are really not supposed to sit on this railing, the top is a row of very uncomfortable spikes.

Top Tip

When you run into a rule that keeps you from doing what you need to, don't just ignore it. That can get you into lots of trouble. Politely ask the gatekeeper, who enforces the rule, if there is not an exception that might apply in your case. If the gatekeeper cannot think of one, maybe someone else can.

9

Travel in Holland

Amsterdam Central Station

BY CAR

Renting a car is easy, but using it is another matter. Rush-hour traffic is notoriously bad. Finding a parking place is mission impossible. If you think you have found one, it is wise to check again. Chances are, it is illegal to park there – otherwise it would not be empty.

Apart from the question of traffic and parking, the differences in Dutch traffic regulations make it more probable that foreign drivers will be involved in an accident. The two major differences are bicycles and right-of-way.

Holland has the largest number of bicycles per capita in the world, with one for every inhabitant – all 16 million of them! By the year 2000 the total number of kilometres per year travelled by bicycle is expected to reach 14 billion, so unless you are used to them, you are a major risk to all the bicycles on the road. Remember, they have equal traffic rights with cars and lorries. Cars must yield to bicycles when bikes have the right-of-way. The biggest problem with bikes for foreign drivers is in making a right turn. Bicycle paths run between the street and the pavement. A right turn takes you across the bicycle path and you have to constantly remind yourself to look for bikes before turning right. Through bicycle traffic has the right-of-way; cars turning right have to yield to it.

Right-of-way at unmarked intersections – and there are quite a few – is another hazard for foreign drivers. Cars coming from the right have the right-of-way. Some drivers take this to the extreme and do not even look left. A collision with crossing traffic is not your only danger here. If you are too cautious at intersections and slow 'unnecessarily' you can be hit from behind by someone who saw that you had the right-of-way and assumed that you would take it.

PUBLIC TRANSPORT

Holland is a small country. It is only two hours by train from Amsterdam to the northernmost part of the country and only two-and-a-half hours to the southernmost part. Public transport spares you the inconvenience and risk of driving yourself. There are two trains per hour between most stations and at least four trains per hour between major cities in the west of the country like Utrecht, Amsterdam, Rotterdam and The Hague. With over 350 stations spread throughout the country, together with the extensive bus network, public transport can take you anywhere you want to go.

Top Tip

You don't have to pay full price to travel by train. The Dutch certainly don't! For bus, tram and metro, buy a *strippenkaart* (strip ticket). They are available at train stations, post offices, tobacconists, hotels and the service counters of big department stores.

Euro domino passes offer unlimited train, bus, metro and tram travel throughout Holland for tourists. *Zomertoer* (Summer Tour) passes offer the same to everyone, but only in the summer months (June-August). *Rail Idee* packages offer do-it-yourself tours to major tourist attractions from a kit. The *zomerzwerfkaart* (The Summer Wander Ticket) offers unlimited travel on the long-distance bus network in the summer. If you are taking the train with children (4-11), buy them a *Railrunner* ticket. It is valid all day for travel with a paying adult. Ask for details at any train station or VVV (Tourist Information Office). Brochures with the most current details are available in English.

If you are not going to be met at the station when travelling by train, be sure to purchase a *treintaxi* ticket at the same time you buy your train ticket. For a low fixed price per person the train taxi will pick you up at home or take you from the station to your final destination.

BY BIKE

Holland is excellent biking country. It is flat! (Except for the south-east corner.) The only hills that you are likely to encounter are the ones that take you up to the level of the bridge that crosses the waterway you have been riding next to. You can take all of them sitting down. Most roads have a clearly marked bike path, and there are special traffic lights and route markers for bikes as well.

Bikes are a part of the traffic flow. They have to stay on the bike path (where there is one), observe traffic lights and signs and give turn signals: your left arm fully extended to turn left and your right arm fully extended to turn right.

'Excellent biking country'

Y ou can rent a bike at most larger train stations and at some bicycle shops. A reservation is recommended.

BY BOAT

B ecause there is water everywhere you go in Holland boating around the country is quite easy. There are 6,340 kilometres (3,940 miles) of waterways, of which 35% are navigable by ships of 100 metric tons and larger. While there are not as many boat rental agencies as there are car rental companies, boat rentals are easy to arrange.

F or pleasurecraft under 15 metres (50 feet) that cannot go faster than 20 kilometres per hour (12.5 miles per hour) you do not need a *vaarbewijs* (boating licence). These type of small, shallow-draft, low-masted craft are not only cheaper to rent, but will also take you to places that are inaccessible to larger craft. The canals coexist with the regular road and rail network and are crossed by one bridge after another. Not only do you have to be concerned with how shallow and narrow a canal is, but also about how low the bridges over the canal are and whether they open or not.

W aiting for bridges to open to let your tall ship pass can take up a large part of your trip. Some bridges only open once an hour. Some can only be opened during business hours, and some are closed all weekend. If your boat is lower than the bottom of the bridge, you do not have to wait.

W hen you pass under a bridge and the bridge-keeper drops a wooden shoe down to you on a line, it is for you to put in your tip for working the bridge. Coins, not paper money are the rule here, but bigger coins are better.

If you want to fish from your boat, a *visakte* (fishing licence) is required for everyone over 16. A licence can be picked up at any post office. Don't leave port without it, if you plan to drop a line in the water.

INSURANCE

Don't ignore the offer to insure whatever you are renting in Holland. The Dutch are not a litigious people. Instead, they insure themselves for every possibility and let the insurance companies fight it out over who pays whom for damages. If you are not insured, you are personally responsible for any damages then and there.

10

The Dutch Language & Useful Expressions

Holland's multi-cultural population

Unless you are willing to put a lot of effort into learning Dutch, there is no real need to learn more than a few phrases. Three-quarters of the population speaks English and those who do, speak it very well. English is taught from the start of secondary school. English-language films and TV programmes are shown in the original language with Dutch subtitles. Many of the smart machines that you will have to deal with – like ATMs, public phones, ticket dispensers for buses and trains – can present their menus in English as well as German, French and Dutch.

A little effort, however, goes a long way. Learning a few courtesy phrases such as 'please' and 'thank you' will garner you compliments and goodwill.

please	*alstublieft* (Ahl's two bleeft)
thank you	*dank u wel!* (dongk ooh well)
Yes, please	*Ja, graag* (yah, hrog)
No, thank you	*nee, dank u* (neigh, dongk ooh)

The only time that you will encounter a problem with the language is with signs. You cannot ask a monolingual sign for a translation. If it knew English, it would have said so already. The list below contains a number of the more important signs that you will encounter.

Alleen gepast geld	Correct change only (On a vending machine)
Gebruik van wagen en tassenhaak is verplicht	The use of a shopping trolley and shopping bag hook is required (see chapter 6)
Consumptie verplicht	Purchase of something to eat or drink required (Often found on or near tables belonging to a cafe or snackbar.)
Defect	Out of Order

Duwen	Push
EHBO	First Aid
Geen drinkwater	Water is not potable
Geen open vuur	No open fires or lights
Geen rijwielen plaatsen	Bicycle parking prohibited
Geen toegang	No Admittance
Lichting __ is geschied	Pick-up (a number from 1 to 6) has been made. (1 - Monday, 2 - Tuesday, 3 - Wednesday, 4 - Thursday, 5 - Friday, 6 - Saturday. – On a post box at the bottom right corner)
Neem hier uw volgnummer	Take a number
Niet aanraken a.u.b.	Do not touch, please (In a museum or exhibition)
Nooduitgang	Emergency Exit
Opruiming	Clearance sale
Overige bestemmingen	Other destinations – not local mail (On a post box. Most likely the slot you want.)
Pas geverfd	Fresh Paint!
Pas op, geverfd!	Look out! Just painted!
Streekpost (zie boven)	Local mail (see above for a list of postal codes that qualify as local) [On a post box, above the left slot for depositing mail]
Stunt	Sale Price (Sometimes referred to in the trade as a 'loss leader')

Trekken	Pull
Twee halen, een betalen	Buy one, get one free
UIT	EXIT
Uitverkoop	Clearance sale
Verboden fietsen te plaatsen	Bicycle parking prohibited
Winkelen met mandje verplicht	The use of a shopping basket is required. (see chapter 6)

Unlike the Germans and French, who dub all the films and TV shows that they buy from foreign producers, the Dutch – and they buy quite a few – leave the original soundtrack in place and add subtitles. You can always tell when they missed the point, because there is a miss-match between the soundtrack and the subtitles. It does not happen very often, but just often enough to remind you that no matter how good a Dutchman's English sounds, there is still a chance that what you said may not be understood correctly.

Always try to be just a bit more precise in the way you say things than you would be at home. Slang expressions, proverbs and puns are the most likely to get you into trouble.

Facts About Holland

Holland is bordered to the north and west by the North Sea, to the east by Germany and to the south by Belgium. It has an area of 41,526 square kilometres. (See map p. 8)

The highest point in Holland is the Vaalserberg Hill which soars to 321 metres above sea-level. By contrast, almost 25% of the total area of the country lies, and 60% of the population lives, below sea level.

The capital city is Amsterdam which has a population of 1.1 million, although the seat of government is at The Hague (Den Haag), which has a population of around 700,000. Other major cities include Rotterdam (1 million), Utrecht (550,000) and Eindhoven (400,000).

Holland's Climate

The North Sea has a great effect on the climate of Holland. The table below gives the average seasonal temperatures (Celsius) and the number of rainy days taken at De Bilt, near Utrecht.

Dec-Feb			Mar-May			Jun-Aug			Sep-Nov		
High	Low	Rain	High	Low	Rain	High	Low	Rain	High	Low	Rain
5.3	−0.2	34	12.8	3.9	33	21.0	11.2	31	15.8	6.3	34

Holland is predominantly Christian, although the majority of people are no longer members of a particular church. There are growing numbers of Hindus and Moslems as a result of the settlements reached with former colonies after the Second World War, especially Indonesia and the Caribbean countries of Suriname and Netherlands Antilles. The constitution guarantees freedom of religion.

The Dutch currency is the guilder (abbreviated to f, Fl, NLG, Hfl and Gld) which is divided into 100 cents. It consists of NLG1000, NLG250, NLG100, NLG25 and NLG10 notes and NLG5, NLG2.50, NLG1 (100 cents), 25 cents, 10 cents and 5 cents coins. Credit cards are widely accepted throughout the Netherlands.

Holland ranks number one in Europe in the use of plastic money. 91% of the Dutch have one form or another of plastic money. In second-place Germany, only 57% have plastic money.

Most shops are open Monday-Friday 8.30/9.00 a.m.–5.30/6.00 p.m., Saturday 8.30/9.00 a.m.–4.00/5.00 p.m. with some staying open late on Thursday or Friday evenings. Nearly all shops, however, close one morning, afternoon or whole day each week. In Amsterdam the shops are allowed to stay open seven days a week until 10.00 p.m. and in tourist areas shopping hours tend to be longer.

Banks are open Monday-Friday 9.00 a.m.–4.00/5.00 p.m. (sometimes also on late-night shopping evenings). Post Offices open Monday-Friday 8.30 a.m.–5.00 p.m. and often on Saturday 8.30 a.m.–12 noon. The post boxes are red and can be found on main streets as well as the post office.

Holland uses the metric system of weights and measures.

Traffic in Holland drives on the right. There are no toll roads, and just one toll tunnel and one toll bridge. There is an extensive rail system. Municipal and regional transport mainly uses buses and trams, although there are metro systems in Amsterdam and Rotterdam. For more details of transport systems, see chapter 9.

There are both coin and card-operated telephones in Holland. The former take 25 cent, 1NLG and 2.50NLG. Cards for the latter may be purchased at Primafoon (the Dutch Telecom outlet), post offices, stations, Tourist Information offices and tobacconists as well as some stores. The emergency telephone number is 112 (as of March 1997) for calling police, fire or medical assistance.

Compulsory full-time education begins at five years of age and ends at 16 years of age, although those who leave at 16 and do not take up an apprenticeship must continue in part-time education for one year.

English is widely spoken together with German and to a lesser extent French. English-language newspapers are widely available.

Holland was a neutral country in both World Wars, but was invaded and subsequently occupied by Germany in 1940.

Holland is the world's largest exporter of cheese, butter and powdered milk; Holland is also the world's largest beer exporting country. Of all the distribution centres in Europe, some 44% are located in Holland.

The port of Rotterdam is the world's leading port in terms of total cargo handled. Together with Amsterdam, it handles 37% of all European Union seaborne imports.

In 1995, Holland exported 370,000,000 guilders ($224,250,000) worth of cut flowers to Great Britain and 117,000,000 guilders ($71,000,000) to the United States.

The Dutch Language

Dutch is the first language of more than 21 million Dutch and Flemish people, and is one of the nine official languages of the European Union. There are 60,000 Dutch speakers in northwest France. Dutch is spoken in the Netherlands Antilles, Aruba and Suriname, chiefly as the language of government and education. Historical links mean that Dutch is mostly used in Indonesia by lawyers, the military and historians. Seventeenth-century Dutch dialects provided the basis for Afrikaans, which is spoken in South Africa. Frisian is spoken as a second language in the province of Friesland. This minority language is the first language of around 400,000 Frisians and has much in common with languages such as English.

The Reformation gave rise to a divide in the Netherlands. The area north of a line running roughly from the province of Zeeland in the south-west to the province of Groningen in the north-east was predominantly Protestant, while the area to the south of that line was predominantly Catholic. The protestant community is further divided into a great number of groupings, such as the Reformed Church, Free-thinkers and Lutherans.

Useful Addresses

EMBASSIES AND CONSULATES

Australia Embassy and Consulate, Carnegielaan 12 2517 KH The Hague Tel: (070) 310-8200

Canada Embassy and Consulate, Sophialaan 7 2514 JP The Hague Tel: (070) 361-4111 Mail: Postbus 30820 2500 GV The Hague

Denmark Embassy, Koninginnegracht 30 2514 AB The Hague Tel: (070) 365-5830 (070) 346-7145. Consulate, Radarweg 503 1043 NZ Amsterdam Tel: (020) 682-9991 (020) 682-5366. Consulate, Westerkade 27 3016 CM Rotterdam Tel: (010) 436-0177

Finland Embassy, Groot Hertoginnelaan 16 2517 EG The Hague Tel: (070) 346-9754. Consulate, Tournooiveld 4 2511 CX The Hague Tel: (070) 364-3628. Consulate, Westersingel 46 3014 GT Rotterdam Tel: (010) 436-2272

Ireland Embassy, Dr. Kuyperstraat 9 2514 BA The Hague Tel: (070) 363-0993 (070) 363-0994

India Embassy and Consulate, Buitenrustweg 2 2517 KD The Hague Tel: (070) 346-9971

Israel Embassy, Buitenhof 47 2313 AH The Hague Tel: (070) 376-0500

New Zealand Embassy and Consulate, Carnegielaan 10 2517 KH The Hague Tel: (070) 346-9324

Norway Embassy, Prinsessegracht 6a 2514 AN The Hague Tel: (070) 345-1900. Consulate, Keizersgracht 534 1017 EK Amsterdam Tel: (020) 624-2331. Consulate, Willemskade 12 3016 DK Rotterdam Tel: (010) 414-4488

United Kingdom Embassy, Lange Voorhout 10 2514 ED The Hague Tel: (070) 427-0427. Consulate, Koningslaan 44 1075 AE Amsterdam Tel: (020) 676-4343

United States of America Embassy, Lange Voorhout 102 2514 EJ The Hague Tel: (070) 310-9209. Consulate, Museumplein

19 1071 DJ Amsterdam Tel: (020) 679-0321

Sweden Embassy and Consulate, Neuhuyskade 40 2596 XL The Hague Tel: (070) 324-5424 Mail: Postbus 90648 2509 LP The Hague. Consulate, Radarweg 501 1043 NZ Amsterdam Tel: (020) 682-2111. Consulate, Willemskade 12 3016 DK Rotterdam Tel: (010) 414-4488

NETHERLANDS MINISTRIES

Ministry of General Affairs, Binnenhof 20, P.O. Box 2001, 2500 EA The Hague Tel: 070-3564100 Fax: 070-3564683

Ministry of Foreign Affairs, Bezuidenhoutseweg 67, P.O. Box 20061, 2500 EB The Hague Tel: 070-3486486 Fax: 070-3484848

Ministry of Justice, Schedeldoekshaven 100, P.O. Box 20301, 2500 EH The Hague Tel: 070-3707911 Fax: 070-3707900

Ministry of the Interior, Schedeldoekshaven 200, P.O. Box 20011, 2500 EA The Hague Tel: 070-3026302 Fax: 070-3639153

Ministry of Education, Cultural Affairs and Science, Europaweg 4, P.O. Box 25000, 2700 LZ Zoetermeer Tel: 079-531911 Fax: 079-531953

Ministry of Finance, Korte Voorhout 7/Casuariestraat 32, P.O. Box 20201, 2500 EE The Hague Tel: 070-3428000 Fax: 070-3427905

Ministry of Defence, Plein 4/Bagijnestraat 36, P.O. Box 20701, 2500 ES The Hague Tel: 070-3188188 Fax: 070-3187888

Ministry of Housing, Spatial Planning and Environment, Rijnstraat 8, P.O. Box 20951, 2500 EZ The Hague Tel: 070-3393939

Ministry of Transport, Public Works and Water Management, Plesmanweg 1, P.O. Box 20901, 2500 EX The Hague Tel: 070-3516171 Fax: 070-3517895

Ministry of Economic Affairs, Bezuidenhoutseweg 30, P.O.

Box 20101, 2500 EC The Hague Tel: 070-3798911 Fax: 070-3474081

Ministry of Agriculture, Nature Management and Fisheries, Bezuidenhoutseweg 73, P.O. Box 20401, 2500 EK The Hague Tel: 070-3793911 Fax: 070-3815153

Ministry of Social Affairs and Employment, Anna van Hannoverstraat 4, P.O. Box 90801 2509 LV The Hague Tel: 070-3334444 Fax: 070-3334033

Ministry of Health, Welfare and Sport, Sir Winston Churchilllan 362-366, P.O. Box 5406, 2280 HK Rijswijk Tel: 070-3407911

Dutch Words Used In This Book

(page references in italics)

Index